EROS IN ANTIQUITY

Overleaf:
APHRODITE, ADONIS
AND EROS
Clay relief cover
for a *pyxis* (box)
Diam. 24 cm
From Italy
Fourth century B.C.
London, British Museum
Inv. D 207

EROS
IN ANTIQUITY

**Photographs by
Antonia Mulas**

THE EROTIC
ART BOOK
SOCIETY EABS
1775 BROADWAY N.Y.C 10019

Published in U.S.A. mcmlxxviii by The Erotic Art Book Society
Library of Congress Catalog Number 78-59722
ISBN 0-913568-29-5

Color separations, printing and binding by Arnoldo Mondadori Editore, Verona, Italy

Erotic art in the ancient world

If we are to seek an understanding of *eros* in art it will be necessary to consider at the same time the motivations and the fundamental points of view which find precise points of reference in myth, religion, rite and ritual, and legend, as well as in customs and in society as a whole.

For it is here that we find a synthesis of what *eros*, which had so much influence and so characterized civilization and artistic production in Pompeii, was to the ancient world, in particular to the Romans and Greeks from the Archaic period of the Seventh Century B.C. to the late Hellenistic period. First of all it is essential to point out the importance of *eros* in the ancient world: its ethical character, or its transcendental significance, or its aesthetic profile, are inevitable features to be evaluated in considering the whole span of their civilization.

To the great tragic poet of the heroic age, Homer, love — like other sentiments — was lived in terms of epic narration. His heroes are portrayed on a large scale; his gods shared the human failings of jealousy, ire, spite, luxuriousness. His, then, was a world of rude and simple sentiments, and love, which plays so important a part in the lives of the gods and heroes of his time, was no different. The beauty of Helen may have been the immediate cause of the Trojan War, but what moves us is the love of Hector for his bride Andromache, the love of the mythical hero Achilles for his friend Patroclus, or that of Ulysses for his wife Penelope.

The Heroes exchanged all due signs of respect and affection, often of very deep affection, yet there is no trace of homosexual love, despite the importance of this in the Greek world. In particular, in the Greece of the Dorians, homosexual love — including love for young boys — had a precise meaning; a meaning which in religion and in law as well as in civil custom, found a precise codification. This form of *eros* was in fact finalized in *aretè*, in what they called civil and warlike virtue.

In Sparta and Crete, as in Corinth and Thebes, each young man was initiated into the art of war and trained in the use of arms by a lover, often much older than he: it is easy to understand how this usage, fundamentally, was neither more nor less than a rite of initiation into manhood. This rite formed part of the primitive sphere of the day. It cannot be investigated using present day theories of psychology and physiology except at the cost of a useless inversion of its meaning. It is also necessary to underline its aristocratic nature, for it was the privilege of a limited élite whose birthright was in fact the use of arms.

Vice and virtue, love, death and resurrection, were the archetypes of myth, frequently used as an attempt to explore the self through the mystic and symbolic rituals which were in point of fact borrowed from myth and transferred from it into daily life.

The Greeks, not only in the Archaic period, but even later in the Classical period, were intimately linked to nature, upon which they depended and to whose rhythm they had to measure their pace. Furthermore, they felt a profound need to rationalize an almost unlimited world of emotivity and of sensation. The theme of *eros* was privileged in the interpretation of this requirement, and it was entrusted, according to the occasion, with the task of striking imagination and fancy through the narration of powerful, heroic, grandiose stories, and descended from this level down through the sensuous to the sensual, the monstrous, the grotesque and to the licentious *eros* of Pompeiian civilization. Here, within the rigid schematism now reduced to the purely worldly level of Rome's mythology, erotism declined into sensationalism.

Sexual union between the gods themselves was seen by the Greeks as the symbol of the continuity of life and at the same time as a promise of the fertility of the earth: in short, it was considered to be a "sacred" phenomenon. The interdependence between Man and Nature (Nature seen on the one hand as an alternation of cycles and seasons, but on the other hand also seen in its wider meaning of instinctive life) can well be expressed through the numerous variants and representations of certain mythical love stories, including that of the goddess Aphrodite and the beautiful young man Adonis. According to one such variant Adonis (symbol of sexual potency) dies during a wild boar hunt while vainly trying to hide under a lettuce. If the wild boar represents the forces of nature to which Adonis succumbs, lettuce — according to the Greeks — caused impotence. The significance of the death of Adonis, dedicated at an early age to sexual pleasure and killed beneath a lettuce, which as we have said symbolized impotence, is thus evident.

Again there is the myth of Hyakinthos, a very young hero beloved of Apollo. In the legend of the tragic death of Hyakinthos, killed by a discus thrown by Apollo during a gymnastic competition, is the underlying theme of the death of vegetation under the too-ardent rays of the sun.

Or again the pretty Pompeiian hamadryads, or tree nymphs. Here the very name, composed of *háma* (meaning 'together') and *drŷs* ('oak') indicates the mutual dependence between tree and nymph, in other words between the vegetable element and its animated concrete representation. And this forms part of a wider Greek conception of nature as an entity having body and soul, and of which man himself forms part.

The deeds, particularly the loves, of gods and heroes were linked together in a superhuman destiny and in exploits, including sexual ones, that no common mortal could achieve, or even imagine. Thus when Zeus lay with Alcmene to beget the mighty Herakles, he trebled the length of night to allow time for such a heroic conception; and Herakles himself was not unworthy of his father in his loves for women and youths.

Side-by-side with the theme of titanic love, is that of courtly love, as in the story of Peleus, who managed to win the love of a goddess though she was desired both by Zeus and Poseidon; or that of Andromeda, enchained and destined to be devoured by a dragon, who is saved by the heroic knight Perseus; or again the episode of the brave Leander, who each night swam across the Hellespont to lie with Hero. Nor is the theme of homosexual love lacking among the gods — Zeus provides an example with the seduction of the young Ganymede, whom he brings home to Olympus. Not even bestiality is neglected: Pasiphae falls in love with a bull and has Daedalus built her a hollow cow; Leda falls in love with the swan Zeus, who appears to be a more-refined relative of that phallic bird which is such a recurrent theme in Archaic and Classical Greek art. Finally, even the transvestite can find his model: Achilles, dressed as, and treated as a girl to flee the Greeks who wanted to take him to Troy; Herakles, reduced to slavery by Omphale, who changes his lion skin and club for woman's dress and spindle.

Gods and heroes were not, however, perfect models, but rather an attempt to transfer to immortal beings the experience of particular and day-to-day things. They were an attempt to mediate a defiance of the irrational or, even more simply, of the unknown, stimulating a new call to thought and to action. What gave true significance to this pattern of balances was the concept of nature and above all of the position of Man in the universe and in society. In this typical anthropocentrism of Greek thought an important place is occupied by the *eros*, with that element of mystery, of imagination, of the superhuman, of sublimation and of trascendent idealization which it might contain. In itself it also interprets substantially that precise and uncomplicated adherence of the individual to the natural movement and rhythm of life itself which is equally frankly explored through other mythological and fantastic inventions.

Take, for example, the animal-man — centaur and satyr. These also represent a highly-variegated but simple world, in which there is no place for prevarication for its own sake even at an instinctive, or worse, at an animalistic level. If animals, such as the mule (symbol of sexual incontinence) or the bull (still used today as a figurative symbol of virility) are often taken as allegorical emblems of human passions and desires, the beast-men are a highly concrete realization of that impulse which consolidates itself in action. Their virility is in fact insatiable: they love the pursuit and the sight of their prey, and their contact with it — everything that fires the imagination rather than satiating. They are almost always portrayed with enormous genitals, frequently they are shown as dancing, playing the flute and running after women while displaying superhuman erections. Like centaurs, satyrs are fond of wine and women, but not of men — for a portrayal of homosexual behavior it appears that the Greeks did not feel the need to make use of hyper-realist figurative substitutions. And if satyrs occasionally commit acts of bestiality, these are no more than a concession to the animal side of their nature. Their life is permissive, vigorous, exuberant, a pagan sensuality of essential vitality which art takes on itself the task of portraying. The most well-known of these beast-men is certainly Pan, the goat-god so often portrayed above all in Hellenistic art. His loves are bestial or, when the prey is a nymph or a goddess, as a rule they are unrequited. Other singular figures frequently shown are Priapus, god of fertility and an ithyphallic figure, and Hermaphrodite, considered and venerated not so much as a pathological freak, but as a personification of bisexuality.

Dionysus-Bacchus, in particular, was the personification of man's earthly passions in their more instinctive expressions. Dionysia (in Greece) or Bacchanalia (in the Roman world) were the names given to the feasts held in honor of this god, in which the original sacred character of the rites — at first celebrated by women only — was gradually replaced by a freer and more uncontrolled sensuality. As god of plant life, which is renewed each spring, and of fertilization, a god thus linked to the life cycle of man and to the mysterious and potent forces underlying both his life and his death, Dionysus was in any case the symbol of immortality. For the ancients, in fact, love was, in all mortal beings, a desire for immortality. And love was still love even in its excesses and deviations, which are simply the effect of the mixed nature of the soul. However, this idealization of love among the Greeks of the Fifth and Sixth Centuries B.C. — love elevated to its most ideal form and to the highest aspects of virtue, beauty and form, as it was consolidated into the sublimation of Platonic love — when it came into contact with Roman civilization, gradually lost its thematic nature.

Starting in the second half of the Sixth Century B.C., as the Attic inscriptions on ceramic paintings testify, with the frequent appearance of the adjective *kalòs* (beautiful), the *eros*, formerly justified and elevated by *aretè* as a civil and war-like virtue, now slipped into abuse and often fell into lasciviousness, losing itself in the soft frivolity of vice and fashion. And such too were the features of *eros* in Pompeiian civilization, which in art as in culture and customs was an offshoot of Hellenistic Greece. Thus deprived of its original and more intimate meaning which interpreted precise customary usages in the light of religious principle, *eros* here frequently declined into disorder. Yet even here love, with all the turbidity and sensuality to which it was tied, was ransomed by art, which corrected its abuses aesthetically, and sublimated by philosophy.

In particular, the average Pompeiian's sentiments were marked by a light-hearted epicureanism which was far more serene and uncomplicated than is implied by the austere definition provided by the founder of this school of philosophy, Epicurus, who defined pleasure as "freedom from pain". In reality, the day-to-day philosophy of the Pompeiian can rather be summed up in the motto "Have fun as long as you can". Pottery and mural art in general confirm this, as do also the very architecture and town planning which allowed for public brothels or for hostelries and taverns as substitutes for them. Again, in the *graffiti* the words *felicitas* and *felix* ("Happiness", "Happy") are to be found continually. For this was the spirit in which life was lived in Pompeii: amuse yourself as long as you are allowed to: "gather ye rose-buds while ye may...". And since sex was considered to be the supreme enjoyment, here is a convincing explanation of the intensely erotic atmosphere to be noticed in the city.

Particularly widespread and frequently represented in art was the cult of the phallus, considered to be a divine symbol and as such absolutely free from any obscenity. It was also viewed as a personification of the god *Fascinus* to whom were attributed — as the case might be — powers of making dried-up plants sprout anew, of making sterile women give birth, and of keeping off the Evil Eye. This cult, widespread also in the religions of India, Asia Minor, Egypt and Greece, was, for the Romans, more than a mere inheritance of tradition from Indo-European culture; it was a true moral need. Thus there was no vulgarity in the impudently natural phallic ritual, but rather a need to curry favor with the god who could protect you from misfortune. The custom of setting up a phallic symbol to protect one's home and even to protect public buildings — a custom carried forward even into the Middle Ages (when it is to be found even on church walls) — was extremely widespread. Frequently, however, the phallus also had a practical function. Phallic sculptures, sometimes of considerable size, were in many cases the spout of a fountain or a sort of gutter for rainwater. When placed in the open mouth of a large mask used as a bird-bath, this mobile phallus acted as a float. It also appeared as an ornamental device on archways, pediments, fountain outlets and gargoyles.

Phallic representations in their more accentuatedly-realistic forms come to form part of the simplest daily life, adorning even objects of common use. If it was current practice by this time to portray scenes of intense erotism on the most widely-varying objects — from the *lebes* (a wine bowl) to mirrors, vases, plates, amphorae, tripods, etc. — the expressive efficacy of other objects, such as, for example, the tintinnabulum (a kind of bell) or the oil lamp, was frequently accentuated by the personification of the phallus in animal forms or by means of other symbolisms with innumerable variations. Common were ithyphallic dwarfs, whereby the Romans certainly showed a certain taste for the ridiculous and the monstrous or, even more simply, for the unusual. Another of these grotesque figurines was the *morio*, a foolish young slave and clown particularly sought after by the Roman aristocracy; or the *placentarius*, the peddler who sold *placentae*, crumpet-like honey cakes also mentioned by Cato; or the *stupidus*, animator of mimes and personage of a horrendous appearance. In all these allegorical types, the least common denominator of the grotesque was the ithyphallic representation. In effect, Hellenistic art poked down into everyday life and thus discovered the beggar, the old fisherman, the peddler, the failed actor living by expedients, the drunken old lady, catching the essential instant which is not heroic and not even mythical, but deeply intimate and human. It is an art often witty in its observations and portrayals, going into the most bizarre and unusual aspects, and sometimes into the aberrant ones, of contemporary life. Yet it slipped into rhetoric and virtuosic excess whenever it exaggerated the image to force greater emotivity out of it.

Finally, another figure of the first rank in the portrayal of the mythical world must be mentioned. This is Hermes. The tendency of the Roman religion to absorb cults and divinities of other countries, in particular of Greece, through a kind of open polytheism, frank and sensual, favoured the diffusion of the cult and of the ritual of Hermes. Amongst the numerous attributes conferred upon this god there was, in addition to that of fertility which he shared with many other deities, that of protector of fields, and that of saving people from the dangers of the roads and from the evil spirits to be found at crossroads. For this reason, images of the god, in the form of rectangular pillars surmounted by a human head, and equipped with masculine attributes, were set up to mark the boundaries between land holdings and along the roads so as to constitute landmarks for travellers. Very soon these also began to appear on the doors of houses with a more strictly apotropaic function. They also appeared in gymnasiums, in libraries and on tombs. When, in the Hellenistic Age, the *herm* (for such was the name of these pillars) lost its cultic nature and turned into a purely-decorative object, embellished and beautified in a hundred different ways, it took its place in private gardens; and it is as such that it is frequently to be found in Pompeiian kitchen gardens.

This was *eros* in the art of pottery, mosaic, mural painting, carving and sculpture. In the art of some of the greatest thinkers of ancient Greece, *eros* was the son of Necessity and was the force that made men live and prosper (Parmenides). Pericles defined it as what citizens feel for their city. Euripides considered it to be the inspirer of the arts. For Socrates it was the search for noble aims in thought and in action. Democritus defined it as the desire for beautiful things. At a later date, love is the principle to which all the thinking of Plutarch was bound, to such an extent that he stated that the first society of Man is a society of love. Among the Romans, however, one finds Ovid's open-minded grammar of love in his *Ars amatoria* and the witty suggestions of Martial in the *Epigrams*. The parable of *eros*, of love, as expressed in figurative representation amongst the Ancient Greeks, is to be found amongst the Romans of Pompeii with a spirit and an essence which are no less admirable.

Opposite page:
APHRODITE AT HER BATH
Roman copy of a Hellenistic
original in bronze
by the sculptor Doidalsas
H. 82 cm
Found in Rome in 1760
Rome, Vatican Museum
Inv. 815

Right:
APHRODITE AND EROS
The goddess emerging
from a shell
is received by Eros
who holds a cloak for her
H. 21 cm
Clay group from Corinth,
Hellenistic
Berlin (East), Pergamum Museum
Inv. 8351

Opposite page:
TEMPLE OF POSEIDON
Detail of the Columns
Sunium, Attica (Greece)

Left:
PAN, APHRODITE AND EROS
Pan attacks the goddess
who threatens him
with a sandal
while Eros pulls at his horn
H. 132 cm
Marble group
from Delos (Greece)
First century B.C.
Athens, National Museum
Inv. 3335

Opposite page:
THE SACRED SPRING
OF CASTALIA
The setting of the spring
and the groves nearby
Delphi (Greece)

EROS STRINGS HIS BOW
Roman copy
of a statue of about 330 B.C.
by the Greek sculptor Lysippus
H. 123 cm
Rome, Capitoline Museum
Inv. 5

Left:
THE SANCTUARY OF ZEUS
Olympia (Greece)

Left:
ERECT PHALLI
Monumental sculptures
in the form
of erect phalli
on relief-decorated bases
Island of Delos (Greece)
Third century B.C.
Opposite page: Detail

Above:
ATHENIAN BLACK-FIGURE CUP
A monster phallus
carried in a rustic procession
worshipping Dionysos
About 560 B.C.
Florence, National Museum
Inv. 3897

Opposite page:
DAPHNE DEDICATES THIS TO ZEUS
A votive marble relief
in the form of a vagina, from Athens.
H. 15 cm
Probably an ex-voto for healing
Boston, Museum of Fine Arts
Inv. 08.34b

Right:
A SYMPOSIUM
The naked cup boy
stands by the couch where
a young man
with a lyre (*barbiton*) reclines
Athenian red-figure *stamnos*
of about 430 B.C.
by the Painter
of the Louvre Symposium
Munich, Antikensammlungen
Inv. 2410

Opposite page:
THE PARTY
A boy on his couch (*kline*)
holds his pipes as he sings
and slaps his knee
to keep time
for the dancing girl.
Hanging behind him
is the pipes' case
Athenian red-figure cup
of about 480 B.C.
by the Brygos Painter
London, British Museum
Inv. E 68

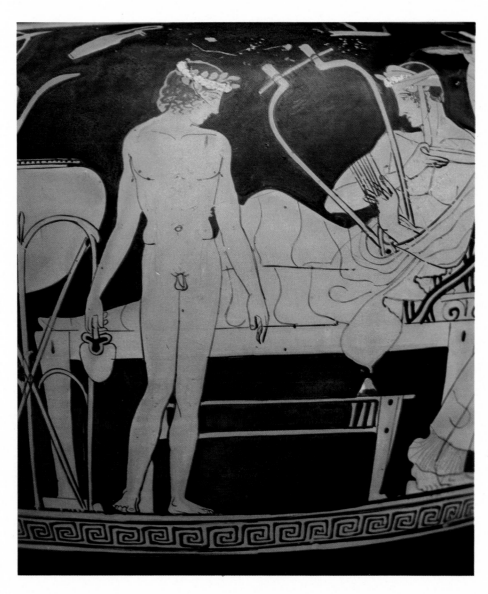

Left:
RED-FIGURE *PELIKE*
A woman "plants" model phalli,
probably for
the Haloa festival
Detail of an Athenian
pelike by the Hasselmann Painter
About 430-420 B.C.
London, British Museum
Inv. E 819

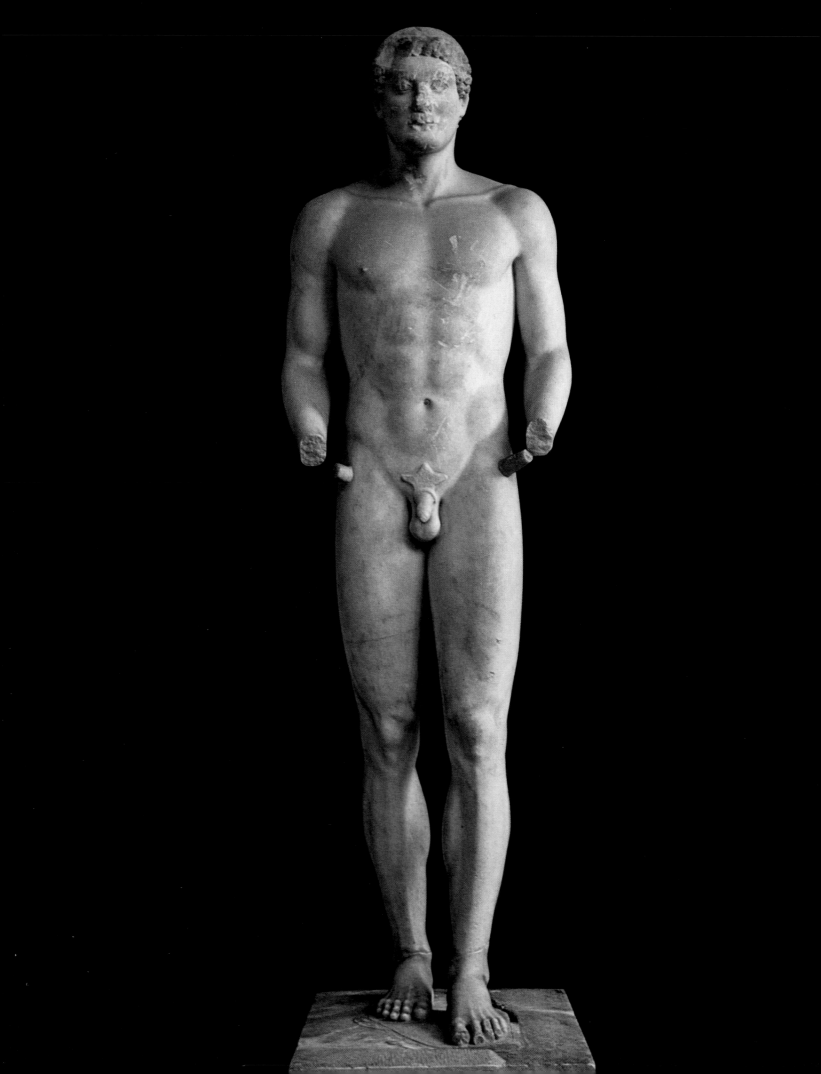

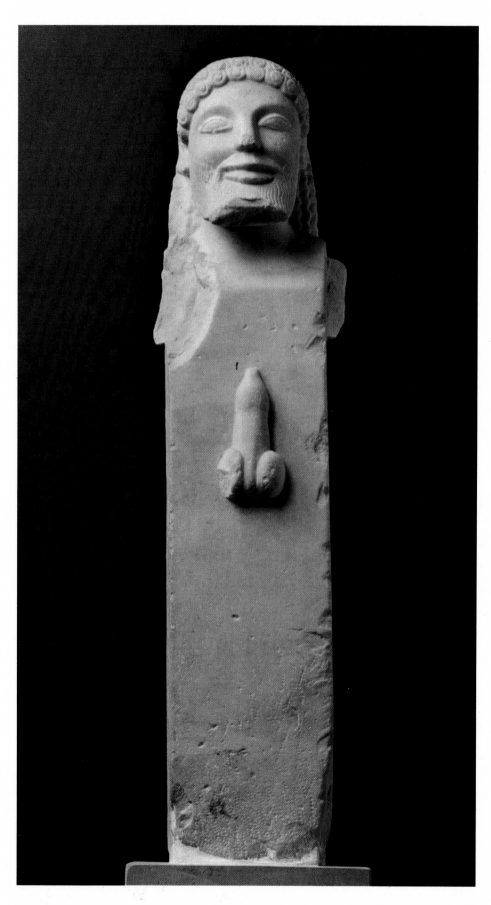

Right:
HERM FROM SIPHNOS
Marble pillar with a head
of Hermes
and erect genitals
H. 66 cm
About 520 B.C.
Athens, National Museum
Inv. 3728

Opposite page:
MARBLE KOUROS
Statue which marked
the grave of Aristodikos
in Attica (Greece)
H. 198 cm
About 500 B.C.
Athens, National Museum
Inv. 3938

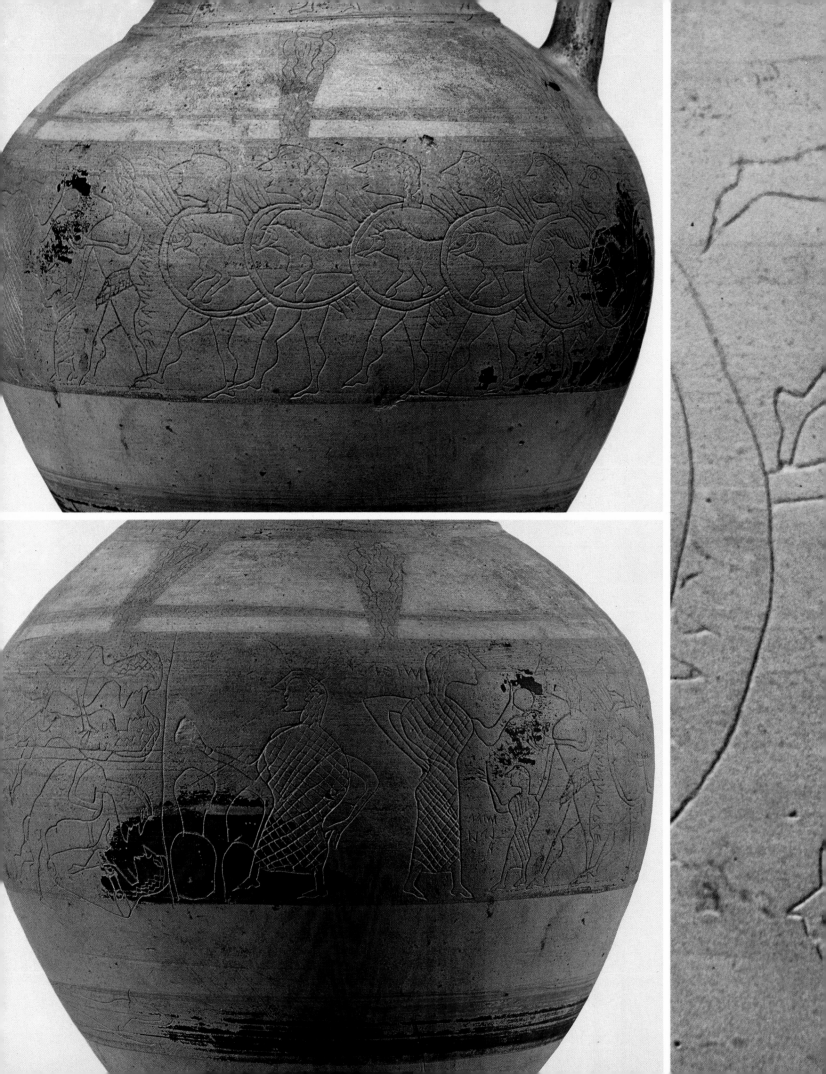

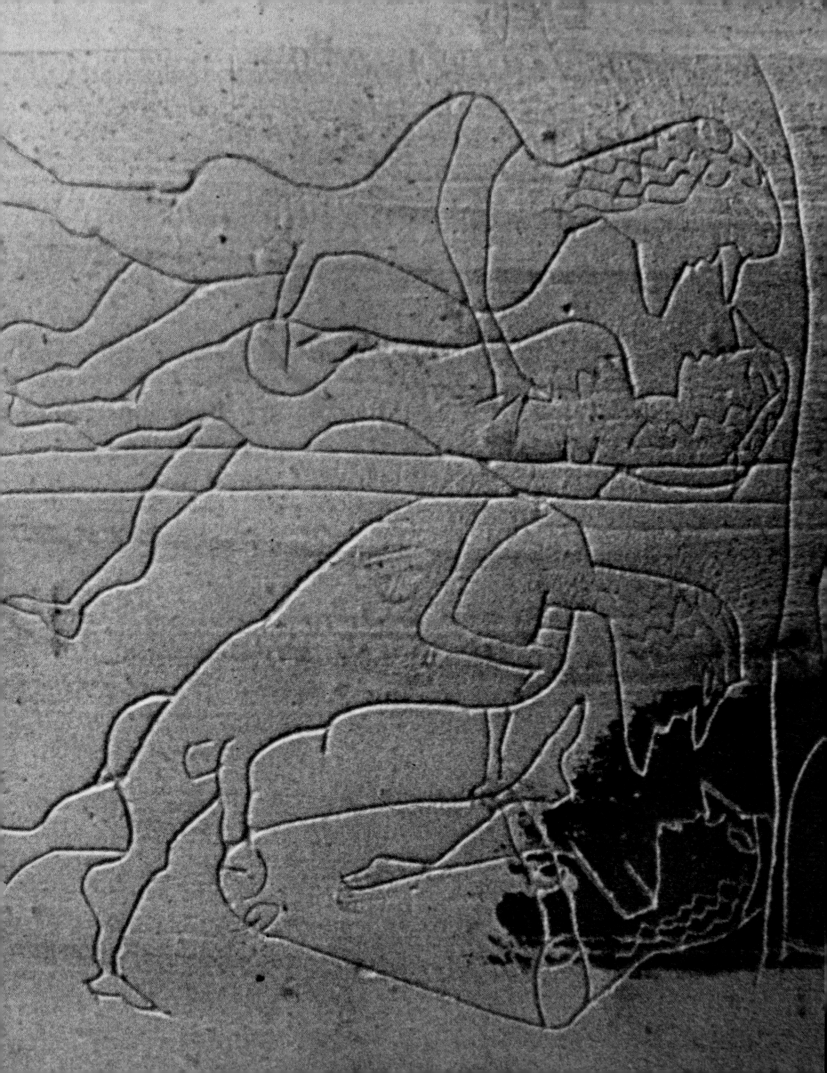

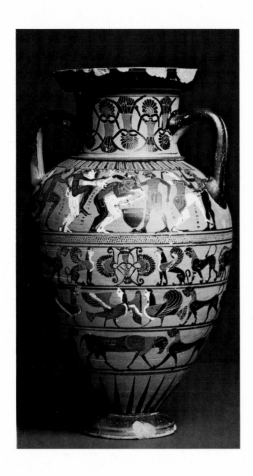

Left:
TYRRHENIAN AMPHORA
Attic black-figure *amphora*
of the Guglielmi Group
from Vulci (Italy)
H. 41 cm
Second quarter
of the sixth century B.C.
Munich, Antikensammlungen
Inv. 1432
Opposite page: Detail

Right:
SATYR AND MAENAD
Attic black-figure *pelike*
by the Acheloos Painter
Detail
H. 32.5 cm
Late sixth century B.C.
London, British Museum
Inv. W 40

Above:
TYRRHENIAN AMPHORA
Attic black-figure *amphora*
of the Guglielmi Group
H. 41.6 cm
Detail
From Vulci (Italy)
Second quarter
of the sixth century B.C.
Munich, Antikensammlungen
Inv. 1431

Opposite page:
PELEUS AND THETIS
Red-figure cup by Peithinos
Detail
Diam. 34 cm; h. 12.5 cm
From Vulci (Italy)
Late sixth century B.C.
Berlin, Staatliche Museen
Inv. 2279

Left:
MEN AND YOUTHS
Attic black-figure *karchesion*
H. 11.4 cm
Late sixth century B.C.
Boston, Museum of Fine Arts
donated by E. P. Warren
Inv. 08.292
Opposite page: Detail

Left:
TWO MEN AT EXERCISE
Attic black-figure cup by the
Amasis Painter
530-520 B.C.
Boston, Museum of Fine Arts
donated by E. P. Warren
Inv. 10.651

Above:
MEN AND YOUTHS
Attic black-figure *amphora*
by the Painter of Berlin 1686
Detail
From Vulci (Italy)
About 540 B.C.
London, British Museum
Inv. W 39

Opposite page and pages 48-49:
EROTIC GROUPS
Detail from
an Attic red-figure cup
by the Brygos Painter
About 480 B.C.
Florence, Archaeological Museum
Inv. 3921

46

Opposite page:
VASE WITH EROTIC SCENES
Attic red-figure *pelike*
akin to the Nikoxenos Painter
H. 34 cm
From Tarquinia (Italy)
Early fifth century B.C.
Tarquinia, City Museum
Right: Detail

Below:
CUP WITH EROTIC SCENE
Attic red-figure cups by the
Triptolemos Painter, from
Tarquinia
Diam. 21.5 cm
c. 470 B.C.
Tarquinia, City Museum

Opposite page:
TWO HETAERAE
Attic red-figure cup
by Apollodoros
From Tarquinia (Italy)
About 500 B.C.
Tarquinia, Archaeological Museum

Left:
KOMOS
Attic red-figure cup
by Douris
Diam. 33 cm
From Vulci (Italy)
480-470 B.C.
Berlin, Staatliche Museen
Inv. 2289

Left:
THE JUDGEMENT OF PARIS
Attic red-figure cup
by Makron
Diam. 33 cm
From Vulci (Italy)
490-480 B.C.
Berlin, Staatliche Museen
Inv. 2291

Above:
EROTIC GROUP
Attic applied-red *stamnos*
About 430 B.C.
Athens, National Museum
(previously in the
Dimitriou Collection)

Right:
CUP WITH EROTIC SCENE
Attic red-figure cup
by the Briseis Painter
Diam. 23 cm; h. 9.5 cm
From Tarquinia (Italy)
About 470 B.C.
Tarquinia, City Museum

Above:
CUP WITH EROTIC SCENE
Attic red-figure cup
by the Triptolemos Painter
Diam. 23 cm; h. 9.5 cm
From Tarquinia (Italy)
About 470 B.C.
Tarquinia, City Museum

Opposite page:
YOUTH AND GIRL
Attic red-figure *oinochoe*
by the Shuvalov Painter
H. 19 cm
Detail
From Locri (Italy)
Last quarter of the fifth century B.C.
Berlin, Staatliche Museen
Inv. 2412

Pages 58-59:
MEN WITH A HETAERA
Attic red-figure *stamnos*
by Polygnotos
About 430 B.C.
Paris, Louvre
Inv. C 9682

57

EROTIC SCENES
Bronze mirror cover (*left*)
and mirror (*opposite page*)
From Corinth
Diam. 17.5 cm
Mid fourth century B.C.
Boston, Museum of Fine Arts
donated by E. P. Warren
Inv. 08.32c

Below:
APHRODITE AND YOUTH
SATYR AND NYMPH
Bronze mirror cover (*left*)
and bronze mirror (*right*)
Diam. 18 cm
About 325 B.C.
London, British Museum
Inv. 288

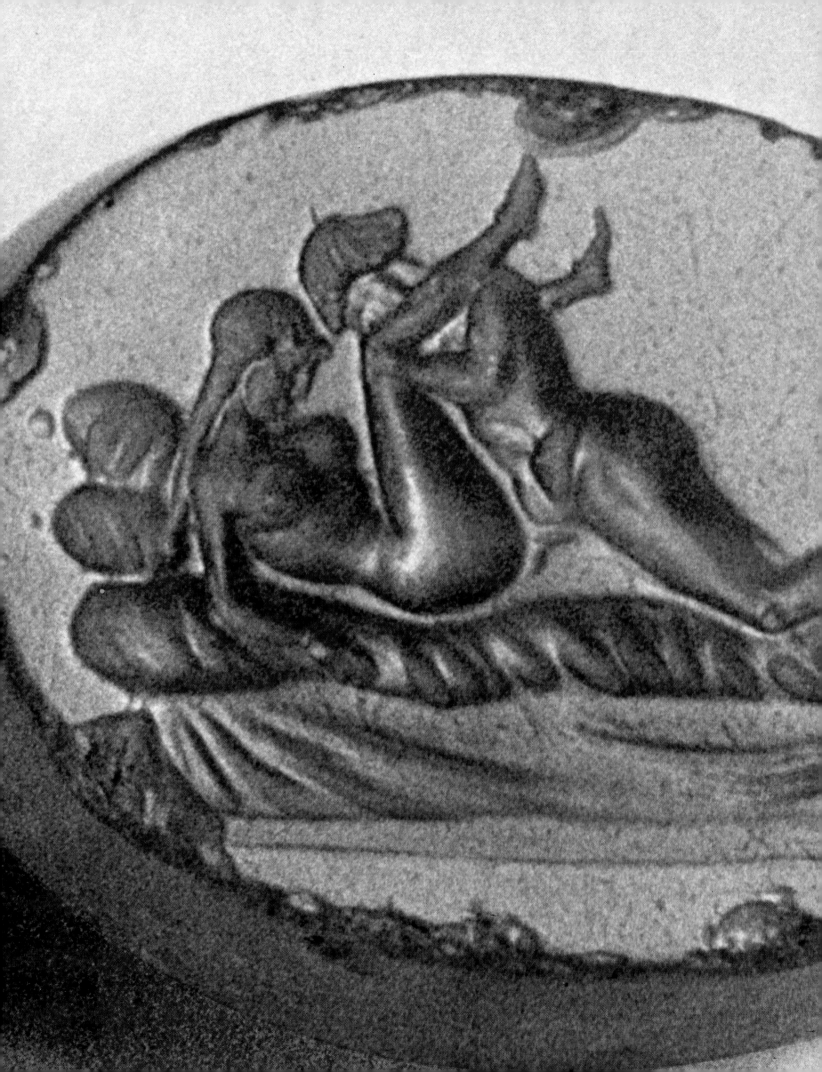

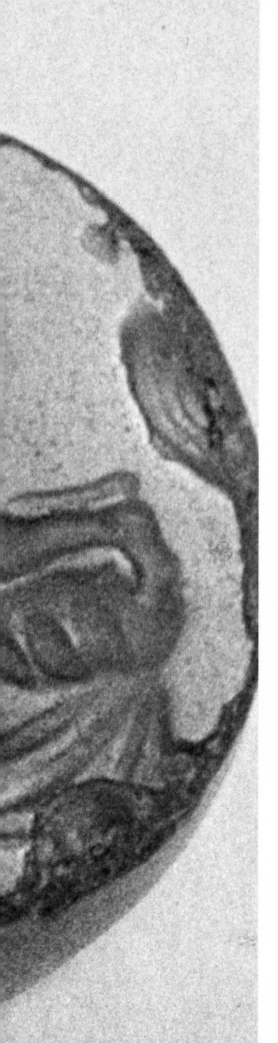

Above:
APHRODITE AND ADONIS
Bronze mirror cover
H. 12 cm
From Corinth (Greece)
Third quarter
of the fourth century B.C.
Paris, Louvre
Inv. MNC 623

Left:
GEM WITH EROTIC SCENE
Scaraboid, blue chalcedony, from
Damanhour
W. 2.6 cm
Early fourth century B.C.
Boston, Museum of Fine Arts
donated by E. P. Warren
Inv. LHG 60

Left:
HERMES AND NYMPH
Bronze mirror cover
H. 16 cm
From Corinth (Greece)
Second half
of the fourth century B.C.
London, British Museum
Inv. 294

Below:
EROTIC GROUP
Terracotta, from Taranto
Third century B.C.
Taranto, Archaeological Museum

Above:
GEM WITH EROTIC SCENE
Scaraboid, discoloured chalcedony,
from Tripolis in the Peloponnesus
W. 2.3 cm
Fourth century B.C.
Boston, Museum of Fine Arts
donated by E. P. Warren
Inv. LHG 63

Below:
HETAERA AND YOUTH
Model for the mould of a
Pergamene vase, bought in Greece
Second century B.C.
Boston, Museum of Fine Arts
donated by E. P. Warren
Inv. 08.33a

Above:
SEATED COUPLE
Terracotta
From Tomb 100
Myrina (Asia Minor)
Second half
of the second century B.C.
Paris, Louvre
Inv. MYR 268 (376)

Left:
SATYR AND NYMPH
Marble
H. 60 cm
From Rome
Trastevere (San Crisogono)
Second century B.C.
Rome, Museo Nuovo dei Conservatori
Inv. 1729
Opposite page: Detail

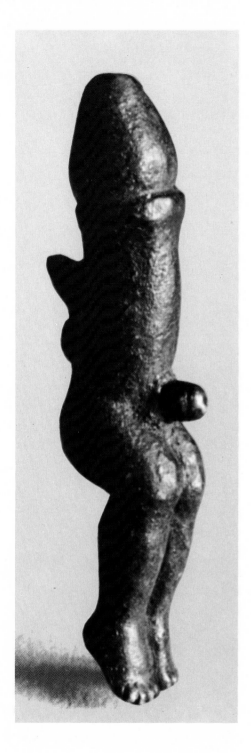

Left:
PHALLUS WITH HUMAN LEGS
Bronze
H. 4.4 cm
Boston, Museum of Fine Arts
donated by E. P. Warren
Inv. 08.32o

Below:
FRAGMENT OF ARRETINE BOWL
Terracotta
40-20 B.C.
Boston, Museum of Fine Arts
Inv. 13.109

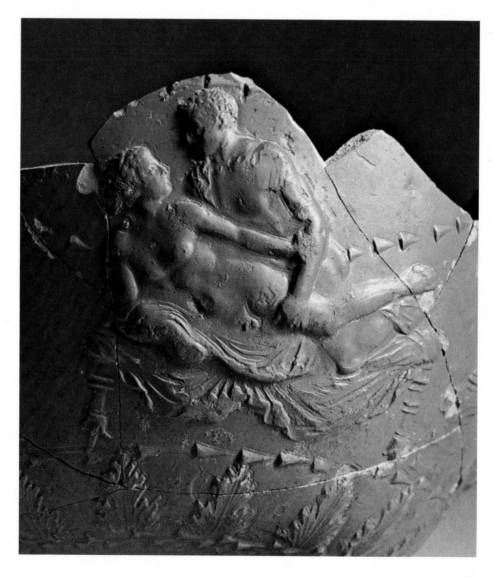

Opposite page:
HERAKLES AND NYMPH
Fragments of a marble relief
Once Coll. Barracco, Rome
H. 40 cm
Boston, Museum of Fine Arts
Inv. 08.34d

Above:
HERAKLES AND OMPHALE
Cornelian intaglio
Second half
of the first century B.C.
Vienna, Kunsthistorisches Museum

Right:
EROTIC SCENE
Bronze mirror
First century B.C.
Rome, Capitoline Museum

Above:
ARRETINE BOWL STAMP
Terracotta
40-20 B.C.
Berlin, Staatliche Museen

Opposite page:
SIREN AND COUNTRYMAN
Fragments of a marble relief,
acquired in Paris
H. 40 cm
Boston, Museum of Fine Arts
gift of E. P. Warren
Inv. 08.34c

Pages 76-77:
ARRETINE BOWL MOULDS
Terracotta
40-20 B.C.
Berlin, Staatliche Museen

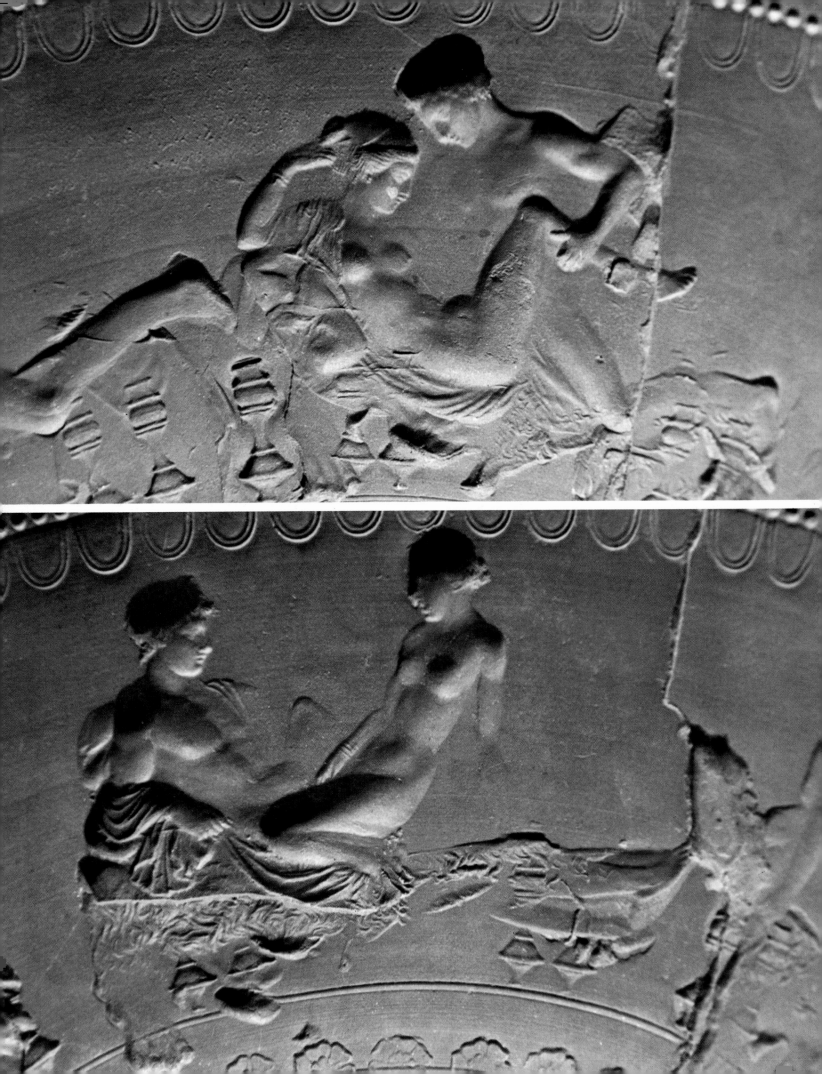

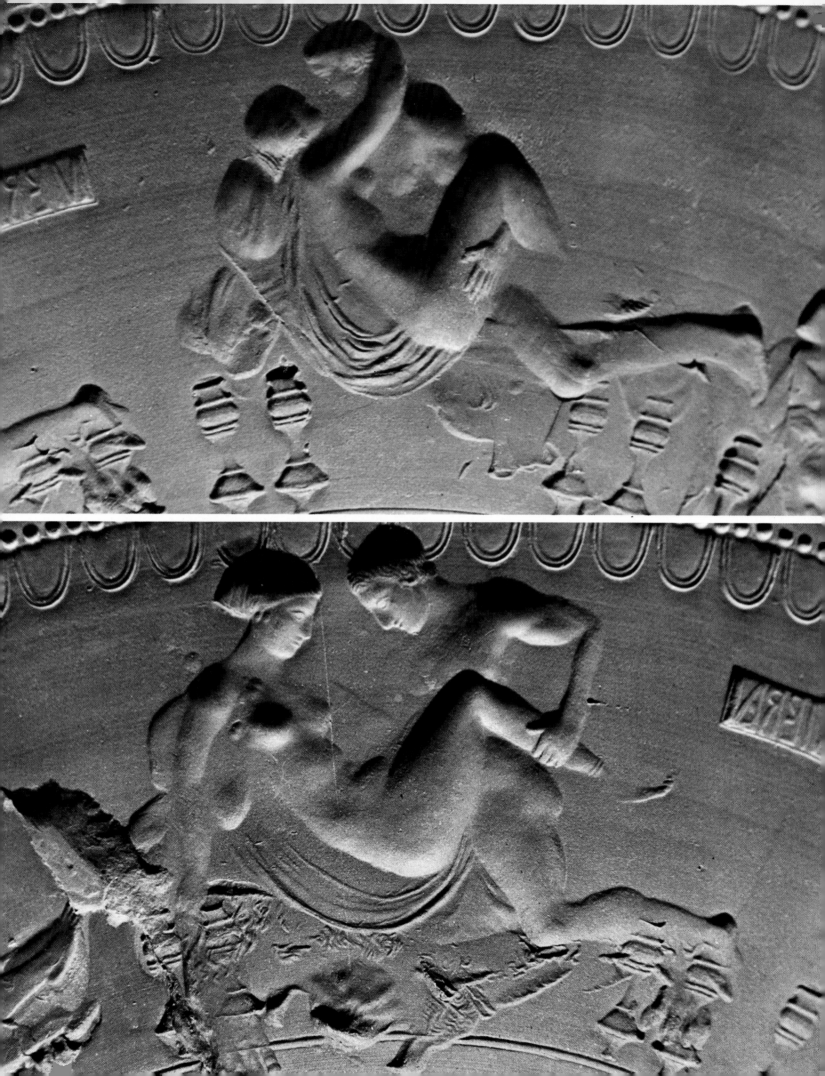

Right and opposite page:
TRIPOD WITH
ITHYPHALLIC YOUNG PANS
Bronze
Diam. 45 cm; h. 90 cm
From Pompeii
(15 June 1755)
Naples, National Museum
RP, Inv. 27874

Above:
POMPEII
A typical corner at the intersection
of two secondary roads.
The large stepping-stones in the middle
of the street allowed pedestrians to cross
without getting their feet wet, and permitted
wheeled traffic to pass unimpeded

Opposite page:
POMPEII
Decorative brickwork
on one of Pompeii's houses.
Set in the wall
is a phallic symbol
designed to ward off
the evil eye

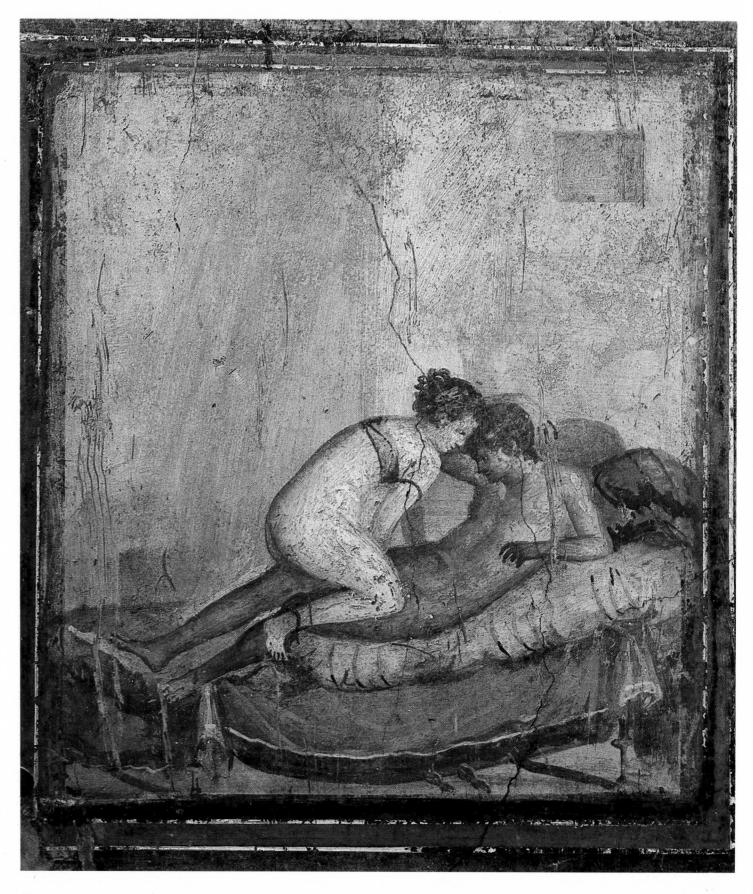

Left:
POMPEII
A fresco from the brothel
with an ithyphallic portrait,
probably that of Priapus

Opposite page:
POMPEII: THE HOUSE
OF THE CENTENARY
So-called
because it was discovered
on the hundredth anniversary
of the excavations at Pompeii.
A wall-painting
showing an erotic scene

Pages 84-85:
POMPEII: HOUSE
OF THE SILVER WEDDING
Another view of the *atrium*,
seen from
the enclosed courtyard
(peristyle)

Below:
POMPEII
Another fresco from the brothel
showing
an erotic encounter

Above:
POMPEII: HOUSE OF THE VETTII
The peristyle and garden
as restored by the excavators.
With its water tanks,
fountains and ornamental statuary,
this is one of the best
surviving examples
of a garden of the early
imperial period (62-79 A.D.)

Opposite page:
POMPEII: HOUSE OF THE VETTII
A fountain in the form
of an ithyphallic figure,
with the phallus
serving as a waterspout

Opposite page:
POMPEII: HOUSE OF THE VETTII
Two erotic scenes
on the walls of a small room
at the side of the kitchen

Below:
POMPEII: HOUSE
OF THE MARINE VENUS
Panel in the Fourth Style
with a marine Venus
and cupids riding on dolphins.
This painting decorated
the peristyle wall of the house.
It has its ancestry in Hellenistic models
and typifies middle-class taste
in early imperial Pompeii

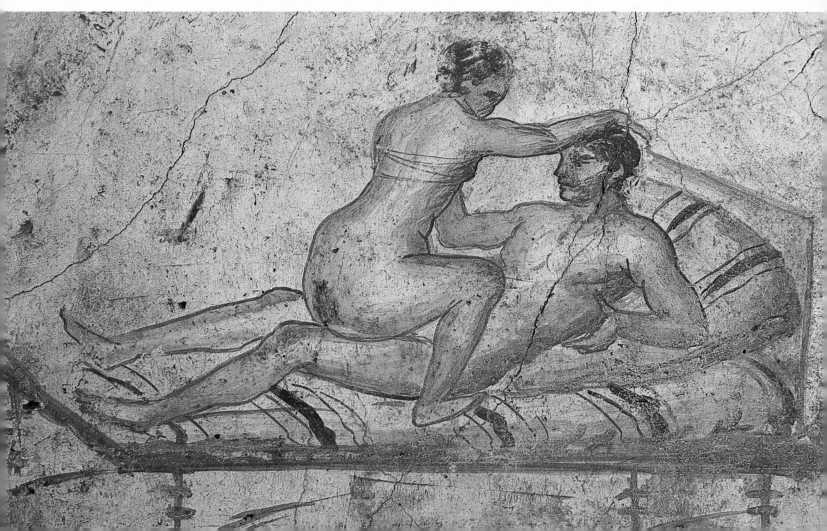

Above:
POMPEII: VILLA
OF THE MYSTERIES
The main *atrium*.
In the centre of the pavement
is the *impluvium* or watertank.
The walls bear traces
of decoration in the Second Style.
The wall at the far end
opens onto the peristyle corridor.
It proved possible
to reconstruct the door on the left
by taking a plaster-cast of the impression it
left in the ashes (c. 70 B.C.)

Opposite page:
POMPEII: HOUSE OF THE VETTII
Fresco in the entrance
showing Priapus
busy weighing himself

Above:
POMPEII: VILLA
OF THE MYSTERIES
Room with a grandiose decorative scheme
based on architectural forms.
Early work
of the Second Style (80-70 B.C.)

Right:
POMPEII: VILLA
OF THE MYSTERIES
Detail of the fresco
showing the initiation ceremony.
To the left, the initiate,
cowed by the whipping
received from a female winged spirit,
takes refuge in the lap of a priestess.
On the right,
a participant in the mysteries
dances naked to the sound of castanets.
Behind her a bacchante
with a *thyrsus*, or wand,
assists in the ritual (80-70 B.C.)

Right:
POMPEII: VILLA
OF THE MYSTERIES
The so-called
"Room of the Mysteries",
perhaps the dining room
of the house.
This rich pictorial complex
is one of the most
outstanding examples
of Hellenistic painting in Italy
(80-70 B.C.).
The paintings show
the initiation of a young girl
into the Dionysiac mysteries,
and in the center of the far end wall
are the figures
of Dionysos himself and Ariadne

Opposite page:
POMPEII: VILLA
OF THE MYSTERIES
Further along the tableau,
a female satyr suckles a young goat
while a young girl recoils
before the appearance
of Dionysos and Ariadne
and the symbols of the mysteries

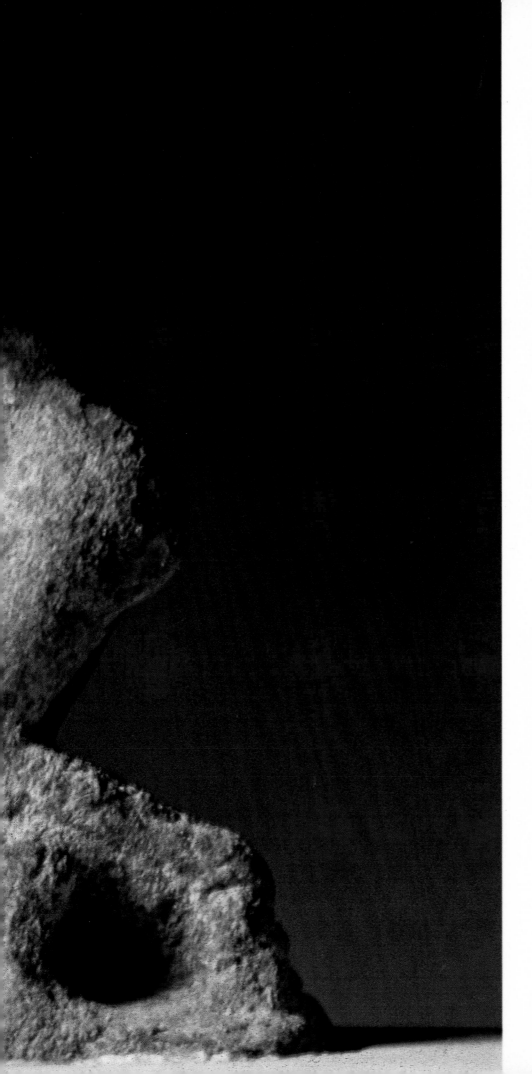

Left:
EROTIC SCENE
Small bronze
4 x 3.5 cm
From the Borgia Museum
Naples, National Museum
RP, Inv. 27715

Page 98:
SATYR AND NYMPH
Marble sculpture
57 x 105 cm
From Pollena Trocchia
(12 April 1963)
Early Imperial period
Naples, National Museum
RP, Inv. 152873

Page 99:
SATYR AND HERM
Detail of the marble
sarcophagus
with a Bacchanalian scene
on pages 100-101

Above:
BACCHANALIAN SCENE
Marble sarcophagus
From the Farnese Museum
Second half of the second century A.D.
Naples, National Museum
RP, Inv. 27710
Opposite page: Detail

Left and above:
PAN AND THE GOAT
Marble group
Detail and whole work
47 x 49 cm
From Herculaneum (Italy)
First century B.C.
Naples, National Museum
RP, Inv. 27709

Above:
SKIPHOS WITH SCENE
OF MAENAD AND MULE
Red-figured Attic vase
9.5 x 17 cm
From Anzi di Basilicata (Italy)
Last quarter of the sixth century B.C.
Naples, National Museum
RP, Inv. 27669

Below:
BAS-RELIEF
WITH EROTIC SCENE
Marble
37 x 37 cm
From Pompeii
Mid first century A.D.
RP, Inv. 27714
Naples, National Museum
Opposite page: Detail

Above:
DISH WITH EROTIC SCENE
Attic red-figure vase
Diam. 23.5 cm; h. 9.5 cm
Detail
Origin unknown
Date c. 480-460 B.C.
Naples, National Museum
RP, s.n.

Opposite page:
AMPHORA WITH EROTIC SCENE
Etruscan black-figured pottery
Diam. at mouth 11.5 cm
H. 24 cm
From the Palatine Collection
Last quarter of the sixth century B.C.
Naples, National Museum
RP, Inv. 27670

Right:
LAMP WITH WINGED PHALLUS
Brown-painted terracotta
Height 4 cm; length 15 cm
From the Borgia Museum
Augustan period
Naples, National Museum
RP, Inv. 27867

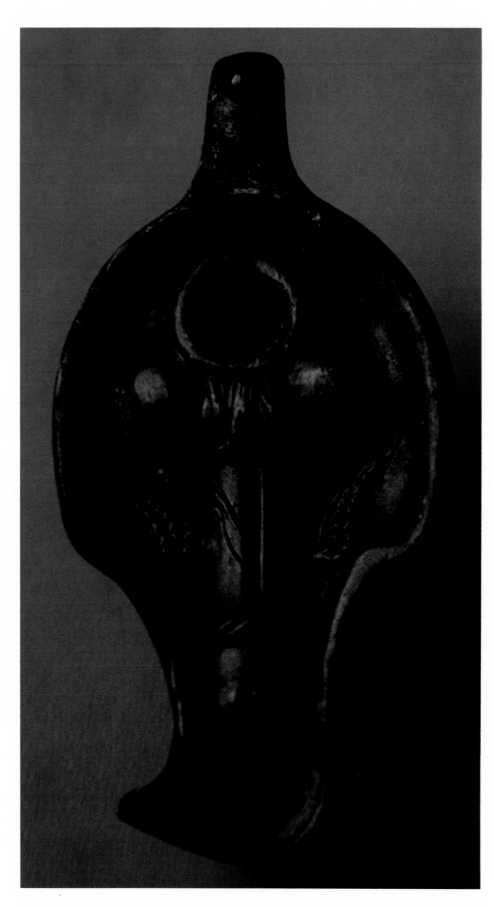

Opposite page:
LAMP WITH SPIRAL SPOUT
AND NO HANDLE
WITH EROTIC SCENE
Red-painted terracotta
Diam. 6 cm; height 2.5 cm;
length 10.5 cm
From Herculaneum (Italy)
Beginning of the first century A.D.
Naples, National Museum
RP, Inv. 27862

Above, left:
LAMP WITH EROTIC SCENE
Brown-painted terracotta
Diam. 5.6 cm; height 2.5 cm;
length 11.5 cm
Found at Herculaneum c. 1873 (Italy)
First half of the first century A.D.
Naples, National Museum
RP, Inv. 110112

Above, right:
LAMP WITH EROTIC SCENE
Brown-painted terracotta
Diam. 6.4 cm; height 2.6 cm;
length 12 cm
Found at Pompeii c. 1872
First half of the first century A.D.
Naples, National Museum
RP, Inv. 109412

Above:
LAMP WITH EROTIC SCENE
Brown-painted terracotta
Diam. 4.6 cm; height 2.7 cm;
length 12 cm
Found at Pompeii
First half of the first century A.D.
Naples, National Museum
RP, Inv. 109413

Opposite page, below left:
LAMP WITH EROTIC SCENE
Red-painted terracotta
Diam. 6 cm; height 2.8 cm;
length 12 cm
Found at Pompeii
First half of the first century A.D.
Naples, National Museum
RP, Inv. 27865

Opposite page, below right:
LAMP WITH EROTIC SCENE
Brown-painted terracotta
Diam. 7.3 cm; height 2.8 cm
length 11.5 cm
From the Museum of Noja
First half of the first century A.D.
Naples, National Museum
RP, Inv. 27864

Above:
HIC HABITAT FELICITAS
Travertine bas-relief
25 x 40 cm
From Pompeii
Naples, National Museum
RP, Inv. 27741

Left:
ITHYPHALLIC DWARF
Painted limestone
11 x 7 cm
From the Borgia Museum
Naples, National Museum
RP, Inv. 27678

Left:
PHALLUS
Sculpture in tufa
H. 39 cm
From Pompeii (?)
Naples, National Museum
RP, s.n.

Opposite page:
GIANT PHALLUS
Sculpture in Nocera tufa
H. 64 cm
From Pompeii
regio IX, *insula* V (30 August 1880)
Naples, National Museum
RP, Inv. 113415

112

Opposite page, left:
BRONZE DANCER
H. 8.5 cm
From Civita (13 June 1755)
End of the first century B.C.
Naples, National Museum
RP, Inv. 27733

Below:
PLACENTARIUS
Two sculptures in gilded bronze
H. 25 cm
From Pompeii
regio I, *insula* VII, nos. 10-12
House of the Ephebe
Last years of Pompeii
Naples, National Museum
RP, Inv. 143760
(same inventory number
for both statuettes)

Right:
HERM WITH HEAD OF BOY
Sculpture in bronze
4.5 x 17 cm
First century A.D.
Naples, National Museum
RP, Inv. 129434

Right:
STUPIDUS
Bronze sculpture
H. 35.5 cm
From Pompeii
First century A.D.
Naples, National Museum
RP, Inv. 27729

Opposite page:
DRINKING-BOWL MASK
Terracotta; 9.5 x 9 cm
From Pompeii (22 May 1843)
First century A.D.
Naples, National Museum
RP, Inv. 27859

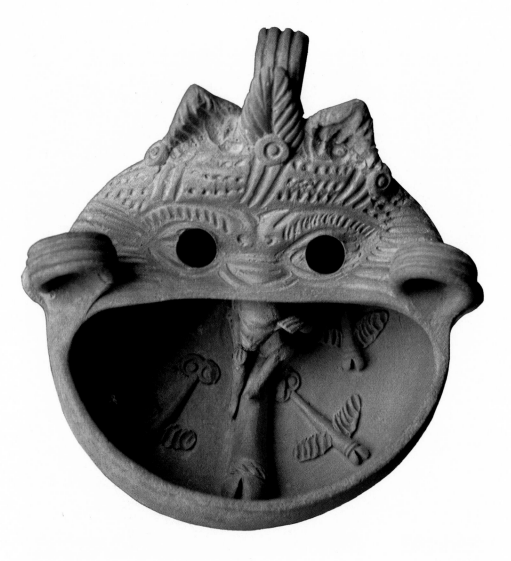

Opposite page, left:
PRIAPUS POURING
Bronze sculpture
H. 22 cm
From the Museum of Capodimonte
First century A.D.
Naples, National Museum
RP, Inv. 27732

Opposite page, right:
MORIO
Drilopos in terracotta
9 x 30 cm
From Herculaneum (Italy)
(11 May 1755)
End of the first century B.C.
to beginning of the first century A.D.
Naples, National Museum
RP, Inv. 27857

Above:
DRINKING-BOWL MASK
Terracotta; 8 x 7.5 cm
From Torre Annunziata (Italy)
(from the excavations carried out
at the end of the last century
in the Battari district)
First century A.D.
Naples, National Museum
RP, Inv. 125169

Right:
DRINKING-BOWL MASK
Terracotta; 11 x 8 cm
Origin uncertain
First century A.D.
Naples, National Museum
RP, Inv. Santangelo 908

Right:
TERRACOTTA LAMP
IN THE SHAPE OF A FAUN
H. 20 cm
From Pompeii
First century A.D.
Naples, National Museum
RP, Inv. 27869

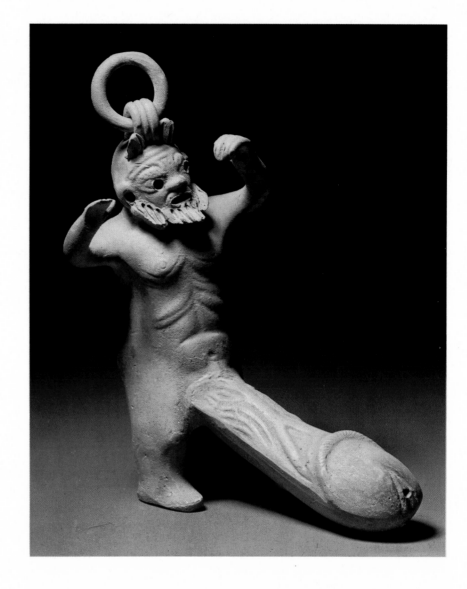

Opposite page:
DWARF RIDING
Bronze lamp
H. 22 cm
From Pompeii
First century A.D.
Naples, National Museum
RP, Inv. 27871

Page 122:
POLYPHALLIC MERCURY
Bronze sculpture
H. 27 cm
From Pompeii
First century A.D.
Naples, National Museum
RP, Inv. 27854

Page 123:
DANCING DWARF
Bronze
H. 13 cm
From Portici (Italy)
(6 April 1747)
First century B.C. - First century A.D.
Naples, National Museum
RP, Inv. 27734

Above:
CARICATURE
Bronze sculpture
6.5 x 7 cm
From the Borgia Museum
Naples, National Museum
RP, Inv. 27852

Right:
THE RIDER
Tintinnabulum
Bronze
Length 10.5 cm
From Pompeii
First century B.C. - First century A.D.
Naples, National Museum
RP, Inv. 27844

126

Right:
THE LION
Tintinnabulum
Bronze
Length 23 cm
From Herculaneum (Italy)
(20 May 1740)
First century B.C. - First century A.D.
Naples, National Museum
RP, Inv. 27835

Below:
THE SNAIL
Tintinnabulum
Bronze; length 15.5 cm
From Herculaneum (Italy)
(2 October 1750)
First century B.C. - First century A.D.
Naples, National Museum
RP, Inv. 27831

Above:
THE MOUSE AND THE TORTOISE
Tintinnabulum
Bronze; length 8.5 cm
From Pompeii
First century B.C. - First century A.D.
Naples, National Museum
RP, Inv. 27841

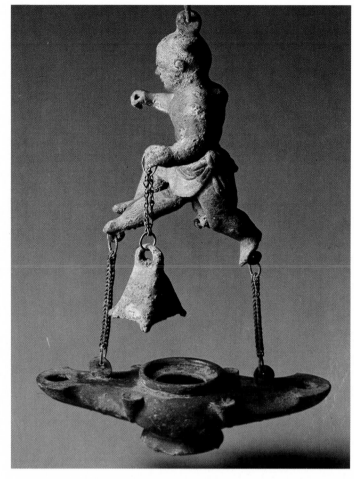

Above:
MERCURY AND THE RAM
Tintinnabulum
Bronze covered with silver foil
15 x 18 cm
From Pompeii
First century B.C. - First century A.D.
Naples, National Museum
RP, Inv. 27855

Above:
THE LAMP
Tintinnabulum
Bronze; h. 26 cm
From Pompeii
First century B.C.
RP, Inv. 27873

Pages 130-131:
SATYR AND MAENAD
Wall-painting
39 x 35 cm
From Herculaneum (Italy)
c. 70 A.D.
RP, Inv. 27699

Above:
WALL-PAINTING
WITH EROTIC SCENE
43 x 34 cm
From Pompeii
c. 70 A.D.
Naples, National Museum
RP, Inv. 27690

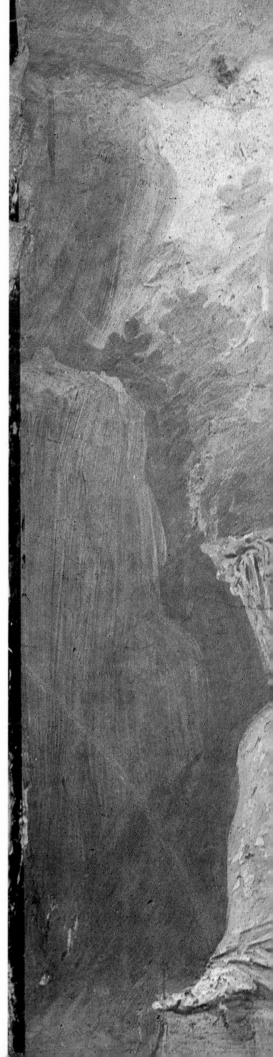

Right:
DIONYSIAC SCENE
Wall-painting
50 x 50 cm
From Pompeii
regio IX, *insula* I, no. 22
House of Epidius Sabinus (*tablinum*)
Last years of the reign of Nero
Naples, National Museum
RP, Inv. 27875

Above:
PAN AND HERMAPHRODITUS
Wall-painting
91 x 143 cm
From Pompeii
regio VI, *insula* IX, nos. 6-7
House of the Dioscuri (*atrium*)
Reign of Nero
Naples, National Museum
RP, Inv. 27700

Opposite page:
LEDA AND THE SWAN
Wall-painting
77 x 77 cm
From Herculaneum (Italy)
Period of Vespasian
Naples, National Museum
RP, Inv. 27695

Above:
WALL-PAINTING
WITH EROTIC SCENE
37 x 37 cm
From Pompeii
First century A.D.
Naples, National Museum
RP, Inv. 27697

Left:
SATYR AND MAENAD
Wall-painting
56 x 56 cm
From Pompeii
c. 70 A.D.
Naples, National Museum
RP, Inv. 27685

137

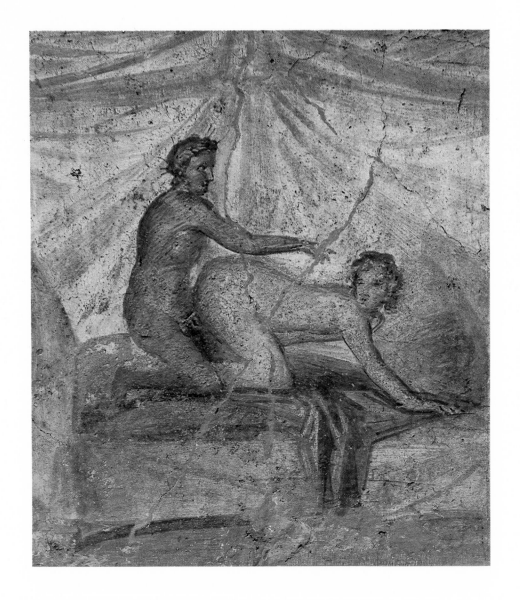

Left:
WALL-PAINTING
WITH EROTIC SCENE
51 x 54 cm
From Pompeii
Reign of Vespasian
Naples, National Museum
RP, Inv. 27696

Opposite page:
POLYPHEMUS AND GALATEA
Wall-painting
75 x 82 cm
From Pompeii
regio VII, *insula* IV, no. 48
House of the Ancient Hunt (*exedra*)
Last years of the reign of Nero
Naples, National Museum
RP, Inv. 27687

138

Above:
WALL-PAINTING
WITH EROTIC SCENE
41 x 41 cm
From Pompeii
Reign of Nero
Naples, National Museum
RP, Inv. 27684

Right:
WALL-PAINTING
WITH EROTIC SCENE
44 x 52 cm
From Pompeii
regio V, *insula* I, no. 26
House of Caecillius Iucundus
Reign of Nero
Naples, National Museum
RP, Inv. 110569

Right:
WALL-PAINTING
WITH EROTIC SCENE
41 x 44 cm
From Pompeii
c. 70 A.D.
Naples, National Museum
RP, Inv. 27686

Opposite page:
SATYR TAKING A MAENAD
BY SURPRISE
Wall-painting
48 x 48 cm
From Pompeii
Reign of Vespasian
Naples, National Museum
RP, Inv. 27693

Left:
MERCURY
Wall-painting
80 x 72 cm
From Pompeii (?)
Reign of Nero
Naples, National Museum
RP, s.n.

Right:
SATYR AND MAENAD
Mosaic
37 x 39 cm
From Pompeii
regio VI, *insula* XII, nos. 2-5
House of the Faun
Second century B.C.
Naples, National Museum
RP, Inv. 2770

Opposite page:
SATYR DISCOVERING MAENAD
Wall-painting
47 x 53 cm
From Civita (Italy)
Reign of Nero
Naples, National Museum
RP, Inv. 27691

Above:
PAN AND HAMADRYAD
Mosaic
25 x 27 cm
From the Museum of Noja
Late the second-early the first century B.C.
Naples, National Museum
RP, Inv. 27708

Glossary

Bacchanalia

Revel-parties given in honour of Bacchus, the Latin name of the Greek god Dionysus. The cult of Dionysus really was of Greek origin. The abundant libations drunk in honour of the god and the frenzy of the rituals freed the participants from moral restraint, and the ceremonies took on a licentious character.

Hamadryad

Tree-nymph who lived with the tree to which she was attached.

Hermaphroditus

Ambiguous divinity who was a combination of both sexes. Son of Aphrodite and Hermes, he/she was regarded and even worshipped less as a pathological freak than as an embodiment of bisexuality. He/she was a strange and sophisticated invention of Late Classicism.

Herms

Rectangular pillars which commonly had male attributes (that you might touch for good luck in passing) and were surmounted by a human head. Dedicated to Hermes, the god of fertility but also the guardian of the fields and protector of people from danger on the roads, particularly from evil spirits at crossroads, they were placed as boundary-stones between estates and served as landmarks for travellers.

Hetaerae

Very clever, witty and well-educated woman: the ancient counterpart to the modern conception of the geishas of Japan. They could talk on any subject (art, philosophy, sciences, politics) and they had free admittance to symposia and komoi.

Komos

Very widespread in the Greek world, komoi (in the plural) began as orgies sacred to Dionysus; later they took on a profane character although they always retained some sort of connection with the worship of Dionysus. Komoi were exclusively a masculine affair; only hetaerae and girl flute-players were allowed access, to entertain the guests.

Lebes

A large metal basin (the word lebes probably derived from the Greek verb "to pour", "to make a libation") which had a wide range of functions in antiquity. They were liturgical objects, used for ritual ablutions and small ones, often of precious metal, were used during sacrifices to catch the blood of the victim.

Maenad

Ecstatic dancer celebrating the rites of Dionysus, the god of wine and fertility.

Morio

Young slave whose job it was to amuse the master. The wealthy Romans possessed great numbers of slaves, and amongst these a particularly sought-after category can be distinguished: the moriones *(in the plural).*

Pan

The goat-god; half-man, half-goat, his face had animal features: horns, a snub nose, goat-like ears and a dense beard. Patron and protector of woodlands and flocks, guardian of the siesta hour. His erotic interests made him a natural companion for Aphrodite and Eros.

Placentarius

A street seller of placentae, *muffin-like cakes of pastry and honey.*

Satyr

Horse-man; a man with the ears, tail and sometimes legs of a horse. His appearance was the invention of Greek artists early in the sixth century.

Stupidus

A character with a rather unpleasant appearance who played a central role in mimes; he was the fool of the company and behaved as such on stage.

Symposium

A drinking party where it was possible, in company, to indulge an appetite for wine, women and song. From this point of view, the Symposium was the equivalent of the Komos in the Greek world. Symposia (in the plural) were essentially an aristocratic habit. Between music and dancing, abundant drinking and games of love, political and cultural problems could be discussed.

Thyrsus

A staff crowned with vine leaves and ivy which was the symbol of Dionysus and was used in his rites.

Tintinnabulum

An onomatopoeic word for the ringing of bells. Tintinnabula (in the plural) are bells which were credited with magic powers capable of warding off the "evil eye"; like the phallus, they were a symbol of abundance and prosperity. The Romans joined the two objects into a composite form, with the phallus as the main part and the bells as appendages.

Plates

Bibliography

Avino, M., *The Women of Pompeii*, Naples, 1967

Balsdon, J. P. V. D., *Roman Women*, London, 1962

Barré, M. L., *Herculaneum et Pompéi, Recueil Général*, Vol. VIII (Musée Secret), Paris, 1862

Becatti, G., *Pitture murali campane*, Florence, 1955

Brion, M., *Pompeii and Herculaneum: the Glory and the Grief*, London, 1960

van Buren, A. W., *A Companion to the Study of Pompeii and Herculaneum*, 2nd ed., Rome, 1938

Carcopino, J., *La vie quotidienne à Rome à l'apogée de l'empire*, Paris, 1938 (English ed.: *Daily Life in Ancient Rome*, London, 1962)

Carrington, R. C., *Pompeii*, Oxford, 1936

Ciprotti, P., *Conoscere Pompei*, Rome, 1959

Clark, K., *The Nude*, London, 1956

della Corte, M., *Case ed abitanti di Pompei*, 2nd ed., Rome, 1965

Corti, E. C., *Untergang und Auferstehung von Pompeji und Herculaneum*, 6th ed., Munich, 1944 (English ed.: *The Death and Resurrection of Herculaneum and Pompeii*, London, 1951)

Diehl, E., *Pompejanische Wandinschriften*, 2nd ed., Berlin, 1930

Etienne, R., *La vie quotidienne à Pompéi*, Paris, 1966

Fiorelli, G., *Catalogo della Raccolta Pornografica*, Naples, 1866

Fracelière, *L'Amour en Grèce*, Paris, 1960

de Franciscis, A., *Il Museo Nazionale di Napoli*, Cava dei Tirreni, 1963

Gabriel, M. M., *Masters of Campanian Painting*, New York, 1952

Grant, M., *Cities of Vesuvius*, London and New York, 1971, 1974

Grant, M., *Gladiators*, London and New York, 1967

Grant, M., *Nero*, London and New York, 1970

Greifenhagen, A., *Griechische Eroten*, Berlin, 1957

Grimal, P., *Les jardins romains de la fin de la République aux deux premières siècles de l'Empire*, Paris, 1943

Hammond, N. G. L., and Scullard, H. H. (eds.), *The Oxford Classical Dictionary*, Oxford, 1970

Harter, H., in Pauly-Wissowa-Kroll, *Realencyclopädie der classischen Altertumswissenschaften*, XIX, 2 (1938), cols 1681-1784, s.v. Phallos

Jashemski, S. A. and W. F., *Pompeii*, New York, 1965

Kiefer, O., *Kulturgeschichte Roms unter besonderer Rucksichtigung der römischen Sitten* (English edition, translated by G. & H. Highet; *Sexual Life in Ancient Rome*, London, 1934)

Lacey, W. K., *The Family in Classical Greece*, London, 1968

Lafeye, G., in Daremberg-Saglio-Pottier, *Dictionnaire des antiquités*, II, 2 (1896), pp. 983-7, s.v. Fascinum

Leppmann, W., *Pompeji: Eine Stadt in Literatur und Leben* (English ed.: *Pompeii in Fact and Fiction*, London, 1968)

Licht, H., *Sexual Life in Ancient Greece*, London, 1932

Lindsay, J., *The Writing on the Wall*, London, 1960

Lloyd-Jones, H. (ed.), *Females of the Species: Semonides on women*, London, 1975

Lullies, R. B., in Pauly-Wissowa-Kroll, XXII, 2 (1954), cols 1914-42, s.v. Priapos

Maiuri, A., *Pompei ed Ercolano: tra case e abitanti*, Padua, 1951, Milan, 1958

Marcadé, J., *Eros Kalos*, Geneva, 1962

Marcadé, J., *Roma Amor*, Geneva, 1961

Marini, G. L., *Il Gabinetto Segreto del Museo Nazionale di Napoli*, Turin, 1971

Mau, A., *Pompeji in Leben und Kunst*, Leipzig (English ed.: *Pompeii: Its Life and Art*, New York and London, 1899)

Menzel, H., *Antike Lampen*, Mainz, 1969

Le Musée Secret de Naples, Paris, 1906

Onorato, G. G., *Iscrizioni pompeiane*, Florence, 1957-8

Pernice, E., *Die Hellenistische Kunst in Pompeji*, IV (*Gefässe und Geräte aus Bronze*), Berlin-Leipzig, 1925

Ragghianti, C. L., *Pittori di Pompei*, Milan, 1963

Robertson, M., *History of Greek Art*, Cambridge, 1976

Schefold, K., *Pompejanische Malerei: Sinn und Ideengeschichte*, Basel, 1952

Sergejenko, M. L., *Pompeji*, 3rd ed., Leipzig, 1955

Simon, E., *Die Geburt der Aphrodite*, Berlin, 1959

Simon, E., *Die Götter der Griechen*, Munich, 1969

Tanzer, H. H., *The Common People of Pompeii* (Johns Hopkins University Studies in Archaeology, No. 29), Baltimore, 1939

Vorberg, G., *Glossarium Eroticum*, Stuttgart, 1932

Zunz, G., *On the Dionysiac Fresco in the Villa dei Misteri* (Proceedings of the British Academy, No. 49), Oxford, 1963

The publishers would like to thank the following for their kind help and numerous suggestions, and for having put at Antonia Mulas's disposal the facilities and rooms of the museums:

Professor Alfonso De Franciscis, Superintendent of Antiquities in Campania; the General Office of Antiquities and Restorations, Athens; Professor Noel Duval, Chief Curator of the Department of Greek and Roman Antiquities at the Louvre Museum, Paris; Dr Piera Ferioli of the Superintendency of Antiquities, Rome; Dr Giuseppe Foti, Superintendent of Antiquities in Calabria; Dr Friedrich-Wilhelm Hamdorf, Director of the Staatliche Antikensammlungen, Munich; Professor Felice Gino Lo Porto, Superintendent of Antiquities in Puglia; Dr Guglielmo Maetzke, Director of the Archaeological Museum, Florence; Dr Barbara Philippaki of the National Archaeological Museum, Athens; Dr Elisabeth Rohde and Mrs Irmgard Kriseleit of the Pergamon Museum, East Berlin; Professor Cornelius C. Vermeule, Director of the Department of Classical Art at the Museum of Fine Arts, Boston; Professor Klaus Vierneisel, Director of the Department of Ancient Art at the Staatliche Museen Preussischer Kulturbesitz, Berlin; Dr Charles K. Williams of the American School of Classical Studies, Athens.

The photographs in this book were taken specially by Antonia Mulas, with the exception of those in the following list:

British Museum, London, p. 46; Chuzeville, Paris, pp. 58-59; E. Meyer, Vienna, 72 on top, 72 at foot; F. Mozzano, Rome, pp. 50, 51, 53, 55, 57; F. Parisio, Naples, pp. 134, 135; O. Savio, Rome, pp. 35, 36, 37; Scala, Florence, pp. 26, 48-49; the Superintendency of Antiquities in Puglia, Taranto, p. 64 at foot.